Bec & Call

Bec & Call

JENNA LYN ALBERT

NIGHTWOOD EDITIONS | 2018

Nightwood Editions
P.O. Box 1779
Gibsons, BC VON 1VO
Canada
www.nightwoodeditions.com

EDITOR: Amber McMillan
COVER DESIGN: Angela Yen
TYPESETTING: Carleton Wilson

Canada

 Canada Council   Conseil des Arts
for the Arts   du Canada

 BRITISH COLUMBIA
ARTS COUNCIL
An agency of the Province of British Columbia

Nightwood Editions acknowledges the support of the Canada Council for the Arts, which last year invested $153 million to bring the arts to Canadians throughout the country. We also gratefully acknowledge financial support from the Government of Canada and from the Province of British Columbia through the BC Arts Council and the Book Publishing Tax Credit.

This book has been produced on 100% post-consumer recycled, ancient-forest-free paper, processed chlorine-free and printed with vegetable-based dyes.

Printed and bound in Canada.

CIP data available from Library and Archives Canada.

ISBN 978-0-88971-348-2

Dédié à ma famille, ma meilleure amie Katrina,
mon beau Nate et à la mémoire de Aidan Kane.

TABLE OF CONTENTS

Belle gueule

Kiss and Tell

Langue au chatte

All Bark. No Bite

Belle gueule

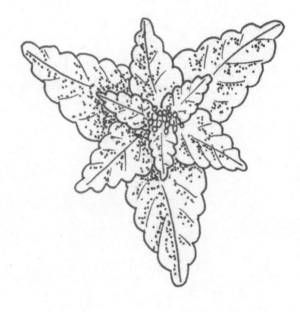

BREAKWATER

I've never been to Partridge Island—
the breakwater's boulders, paired
with the high tide are enough to spook
any good bogtrotter from crossing over.
From Bayshore, it's nothing more
than a green mass, shards of brown
and broken beer glass, NO TRESPASS.
A rite of passage that's right risky
lures pilgrim punks to get drunk,
to tag tunnels with teenage smut,
to cock middle fingers at the coast:
I am a rock, I am an island, I am
campfire singalongs and discarded
thongs, bongs decorating desecrated
gravestones. My high school English
teacher starred in a knock-off Heritage
Minute, Dr. Patrick Collins crumbling
to typhus fever echoed by hipsters
falling over drunk: a part of our history.

DOUBLE-BARREL

Sticks and stones may break my bones but words, words, words
and what's in a name, anyway? Mom and Dad couldn't decide
on a name, settled for two. No hyphen, no compound—a twofold
monstrosity printed on my birth certificate, signed and dated:
the April Fool's joke it've been if I were on time once in my life.

"Jenna," after the brunette from *Another World*, with perm-
perfect ringlets and spaghetti-strapped shoulders, her brooding
boyfriend's "A Song for Jenna." While every Jolene and Layla
and boy named Sue got a proper ballad, all I got's a discount
daytime serenade: on demand, DejaView. Then "Lyn," Mom's
matronymic flourish.

My soap opera namesake didn't matter much in school, not once
the boys began watching porn, having discovered Jenna Jameson
in their daddies' DVD collections or search histories: double DS
are just as good on dial-up. Lucky for me, there were no eggplant
emojis in MSN messenger, only *<Contact> has sent you a nudge.*

I dropped "Lyn" at first, until classmates gave me a nickname;
"Jenna" became "genitalia"—a pussy epithet shouted in the hall,
and I know better than to answer that catcall. "Lyn" made
a comeback, a goody two-shoes less prone to vulgar
nomenclature than "Jenna." Two names are a lot harder to
pervert: innuenduo.

HEAD AND HEART

Mom spent hours beachcombing my head: plucking pearlescent
parasites from my scalp-scape, then crushing them into Kleenex
—the cochineal mix, blood and bug and tea tree oil, tie-dyeing
tissue after tissue the colour of poppy pins come November,
black cherry Kool-Aid, Dad's '86 Chevy to the levy.

I'd sit on the toilet seat, bowed over the sink in prayer: *Please
let there be no more nits or eggs or creepy-crawlies and I swear
I'll never…* and after a week of supplication, Mom gave up
fingering my long brown curly hair, scissoring it off into a Posh
Spice blunt bob, and why they call it a bob at all is beyond me.

When I hear "Hallelujah," it makes me itch—I've had a few
never-have-I-evers and I'm a catechism dropout, and too
often it's Wainwright instead of Cohen, but can you feel
the hair in your mouth, on your tongue? I have split ends.

WORRY DRAGONS

In kindergarten I refused to stay at school, screamin' Jay Hawkins till teacher called home. I'd get on the school bus by myself, Dad driving behind like a tug ushering a ship to dock while I watched from the emergency door. We pulled into Millidgeville North and Dad turned the rusting "Blue Beater" around, the Chevy Cavalier, my cavalry, fading into fog. That's when I went full-Joplin: projecting heartbreak to the second floor, the office, tears sputtering like that faucet in the girl's washroom with its hard water buildup. Pigtails like Baby Spice and chin twitching à la swatted fly before the cat eats it up, my *alouette, gentille alouette* was half-hearted. The principal advised my parents to enroll me in a program for the anxious at the Mercantile Centre. A pretty lady with brown hair, but curly—not frizzy and thick like mine—said I have Worry Dragons. We coloured the dragons with soft edges, drew faces like puppies and *Why should I worry? Why should I care?* The therapist called me a hardboiled egg and peeled away the shell and membrane, little by little. I didn't like hardboiled eggs. Once she told Mom to send me to Tim's for a treat without enough change to pay. The cashier took the shiny toonie with a golden polar bear, warm from my OshKosh B'gosh pocket. "Do you have a quarter, sweetie? You're a bit short." I'm a bit short of serotonin, norepinephrine. She smiled and let me go with the Timbits shortchanged, tears like damp bruises blooming on the cardboard box.

APIARY

At the bell, all of us kids
swarm the flaking paint
that curls from the metal
framing like flower petals
opening to the noon sun.
Our hands are scratched
from rust spots, palms
indented by the swing set's
chains, the pea gravel after
jumping off—arms extended
not for flight, but for the fall:
we are gracelessly agile,
flexible bodies bumping,
bumbling around the school
yard. The girls get in trouble
for hanging upside down
from the monkey bars,
our shirts slipping down
to show our chests. I flip
right-side up before a teacher
sees me, already missing
the breeze on my belly
and back and breasts.
Swinging back up to grab
the bar, there's a honeybee
and I'm stung. Ben called
my boobs bee stings once,
and it looks like my thumb's
got a nipple where the stinger
sticks out: pink and warm.

SILVERMOUNT CRESCENT

You know the hill, the one with the steep incline and
no sidewalks, crack weeds sprouting from the concrete
curbside come summer. The stop sign at the bottom's
as bent out of shape as I am, tweaked by the snow
plow or bus-stop brats trying to steal it, or both.

Eyes closed for sleep, REM-red flickers go octagonal:
the stop sign, the hill: a recurring dream of Silvermount
Crescent as a sheet of ice, the slope asphalt-black,
lacklustre as the grey sky and just as nebulous. Mémère
and Pépère live at the peak and I must get to their house:

Little Red Riding Hood taken out of the forest, out
of the wolf's den. The Big Bad's barely there, ice fog
obscuring the road, the twin maple trees—now skeletal—
adorning every lawn, the neighbouring bungalows,
and when I try to walk I slip 'n slide back to stop-start.

On all fours, I crawl, naked-palming the ice but making
progress, my hands are cold and wet and my skin
is freezing to the slick like a moist tongue to a frigid
sign post: an icy steel trap gone SNAP. I swear I can see
fur, the pelt I left behind, on my wake-walk home.

RIVERHILL DRIVE

My dad says there were never deer here when he was a child.
Hands anchoring hips sore from the summer he hit a doe
five houses down: the Harley, himself, the ruminant,
all road-rashed. Blasting forced the deer down from the hills
to suburbia. Now winter-thick fawns, sepia against February
snowfall, are as common as raccoons or red squirrels.
Seasonally starved whitetails leave the spruce well enough
alone; we wrap the rhododendron in burlap, regret that ribs
protrude from their flurried pelts. One fawn doesn't make it
this year. The deer track scalloped hearts as they curlicue
between backyards; eyes lashed long and mascara-black
as my sister's as we huddle on the back deck, passing a joint
precariously between mitted fingers. Us, the does, we're wide-
eyed, sending lungfuls of earthy vapours to the snow moon.

SUNDAY DRIVE

In the backseat of the CR-V we sulk, sloth-slouch
with our knees pressed to Mom and Dad's backrests.
My sister and I mimic the livestock as we pass them
by on a Sunday drive: our first family excursion since
the great Timbit tantrum of '01: there's still sugar
creviced in the folding cup holder: our stanchion.

When she was a newborn, my sister and I played
with one of those Mattel See 'N Say toys, taking turns
pointing the big red arrow at the farm animals
and cranking down the lever, listening to the noises
of cat or horse or frog, barely audible over the *snap-
crackle-pop* of the subpar recording. The FM radio's

out of range on these back roads, static like the rip-tear
of the light-up Velcro sneakers that Mom neglected
to buy for the both of us, lucky you. It's her own
damned fault that you tracked dirt inside the house,
pumped up kicks mercilessly mowing down the carpet
without etiquette, without a shoelace of regret.

Dad's solution for when the See 'N Say toy began
to skip, and now with the confiscated light-bright
footwear, was to toss out the problem. The LED soles
continued to pulse through the sheer black garbage
bag as he threw 'em curbside. "Ducks go *quack*, sheep
go *baa*," and kids snivel till the cows come home.

THERE'S AN OLD VHS OF MY MÉMÈRE…

…dead drunk at a *vrai fête de cuisine*, put to bed early, one of her many brothers giving her last rites—*les derniers sacré-bleus*, absolution after absinthe, abstinence and Christ on the cross hungover, hung over her body, arms crossed over her chest like a stiff and the whole family, having had too many stiff drinks, got into Mémère's homemade wine, siphoned it straight from the jug and it wasn't far off from gasoline, and as quick as she's down she's risen at the offer of a cigarette, sheer black pantyhosed toes padding down checkered stairs to sit beside my dad, barely a teenager, playing a beaten-up beatnik of a guitar and gulping swigs of Spumante Bambino between bastardized Cash covers.

MOLLUSCA

I

Periwinkles are best boiled in sea water, algae green shells whirling inward, upward. No matter, no need for butter or batter. Use a bobby pin, toothpick or Mémère's sewing needles to out the meat once the operculum's off. The spiral morsels are dun-coloured, immaculately muculent. One time, my sister and I went with Dad to St. Martin's to salvage sea snails on the beach. Salt and sand scented the truck on the dusk-drive home, plastic pail brimming with *bigorneaux*.

II

Oysters are best bought at the City Market, the dozen in a wooden crate's a bargain. Better yet, buy 'em from the fisherman, pickup parked at the Shell station on Main Street West. Share a swig of Fireball from the flask kept in the centre console. Pépère's hands shake when he shucks now, butter knife bending to shell and palm to grit: more slate than sand. Slurp 'em back and swill 'em like the rye whisky we've been double-digiting all night: on ice, straight down the gullet.

III

Mussels are best chucked out if clenched tight at boil's end. Mémère's melted butter in individual bowls, and we knock knuckles in the pot, grabbing for still-steaming onyx shells, curiously opalescent. The mussels themselves are Tuscan yellow, fringed by a dark flapper skirt. Dunk the meat, fingers too, into the warm milk solids floating among the butterfat. Tongue the fleshy pâté, luxuriate in its mushy mouth-feel, and repeat until there's nothing left but a salt-stained saucepan, a sailor's sunset, nailbeds brined.

TONGUE-IN-CHEEK

The dinner plate is white and square
like the fancy ones from restaurants,
the tablecloth white and oval and even.
There's a small salad fork to my left
and my sister's place is set the same,
tiny utensils for two *petite minettes*
with *bon appetites*, each of us eyeing
the up-cycled jam jars of *racinette*
that we can't drink until O Captain!
My Captain! has his food served to him,
our supper following *tout de suite*.
Here we're given cloth napkins, not
paper, and I hate using them because
they are white and clean and folded.
Pépère made our meal tonight: seafood,
his specialty, the potatoes and fish dish
all white, cut into bite-sized pieces
that barely stand apart from the dishes
they are heaped on. My sister and I eat
the white meat and starch, *les poissons,*
les poissons, hee hee hee, haw haw haw
but Pépère gets the last laugh, smile
all gums, dentures waggling, he asks
how we like our cod tongue and cheek.
Mid-mastication, we pause. *Pardonne-*
moi? He swish-swishes his teeth back
to their proper position, says nothing.
A muffled retch comes from my sister,

running for the *salle de bain* faster
than Mémère can *Ostie d'calvaire,*
Claude, and there's tongue in my cheek
and cheeks on my tongue and it's not
long before I'm kneeling with my sister
over the toilet, the tile not nearly
as comfy as the *prie-dieux* at church.

TURNING BLUE

Do you remember that terrifying live action *Alice in Wonderland* circa 1999? The one where the walrus and the carpenter eat the young, curious oysters and Whoopi Goldberg is a cat—not a pie. The Queen of Hearts' eyebrows were on fleek, her head calligraphied with curving lines to resemble hair and her lips scarlet as the Sacred Heart. Flamingos made for lovely croquet mallets in a pinch, hedgehogs for dodgy balls. Mom left us TV dinners—the kind with cheap chocolate pudding we couldn't eat until we were done the mashed potatoes and corn and soggy chicken. The babysitter's daughter bribed us to eat with the cassette, our reward the black tongue rolling back into a VHS mouth. We sometimes forgot to rewind the movies, metallic whirs and blue screens marking the time until the click-thunk of the reel's start. You cried when Pépère offered us oysters, but they didn't seem very curious to me: shucked in the back shed and offered on the half shell. "Don't spill the liquor," he'd said. I told my grandfather kids aren't supposed to drink and he laughed, pressing the shell to my lips and all I could taste was grit and seawater. I spit it out faster than I'd slurped it in, raw embryotic mollusc spewed into Mémère's garden: a glistening, repugnant slug on fresh mulch. Dad and Pépère sat in the sun, bellies distended with shellfish and beer, the walrus and the carpenter chuckling at their young: curious and blue.

WEEDS

after Kayla Czaga's "Wild Lilac"

The time my mother asked me to help her weed the front garden, I got in an ant hill without gardening gloves and a big black emmet bit me real good, drawing blood, and I didn't cry until Mom pulled on the bug and wound up yanking its ass end off and, even bifurcated, the thing squirmed, mandibles unrelenting. The times we'd fall asleep sitting up, propped against the gaudy 1980s couch with its pastel florals and armrest covers. The time I wanted a refund when my new brother turned out to be a sister and wouldn't stop bawling like a little bitch. I got grounded for that one. The time I tested her love of butter with a dandelion by accident and she showed me how to suck nectar from red clover florettes, us stealing weeds from the backyard before Dad could get them with the John Deere. The time my sister and I got head lice from school and Mom combed through hair slick from tea tree oil with the precision of a surgeon until the second time and she took us for haircuts: *It will grow back fast, your hair's a weed.* The time my mother stopped colouring her hair and it grew out platinum and she somehow looked younger. The time she got dizzy spells and went for blood tests, type 2 diabetes, and every time she pricks her finger to test her sugars I think of the ant's puncture marks on my finger. The time my mother looked frail, cat napping on her lap in the sunroom, early spring after a glucose crash. We've stopped snatching up the buttercups, lawn mower mulching grass with yellow petals and purple stems along with deer shit, the occasional trash scrap from the coons.

IDENTITY CRISIS AT DIXIE LEE: SHIPPAGAN, NB

Twelve years of French immersion didn't prepare me
for this moment, *ma belle gueule,* wanting for the words
to order at a Dixie Lee in Northern NB: *presque vu.*

I batter my brain, deep-fry parietal, temporal lobes
in a freshet of grease. I remove them prematurely, gone
all Shubenacadie Sam and nothing's near done;

not winter, not the *langue* of a drive home, not the knot
of hunger for *Acadie,* Gabriel to my Evangeline: lost
and found long enough to go bad at the back of the fridge

behind the Baxter's and Becel. My fast-food French sits
heavy in the belly, stains the clamshell take-away box
with imprints like wet asses on patio chairs. It's not an easy

clean up, I've cracked into the lobster *sans les flyers,*
fingers fishy, hands éperlan flopping useless as my tongue
over basic, back-home vocabulary—*comment ça flip?*

JELLYFISH

Have you ever dissected a beached jellyfish? Come jelly season,
arctic reds of all sizes polka-dot the Shediac shoreline magenta,
violet bells shielding unwitting soles from stinging tentacles,
their colourful lion's manes tangled like wet, salt-saturated hair.
Jellies feel like seaweed at your ankles, brushing your thighs
while you swim: passively aggressive until they're beach bound.
A piece of driftwood or a shovel will suffice to flip the sea jelly,
revealing its oral surface. Nematocysts like hypodermic needles
are active even after they're little more than deflated soufflés.

FAMILLE

You hate roses, their damask scent of formaldehyde, methanol:
paper boats lure schoolboys into the Saint John River.

The maple in the backyard sheds its leaves prematurely, determinedly.
Choleric, it digests itself—yellow bile seeping through dappled bark.

Menstrual synchrony's a bitch in a household of women: some sheets
never see the line, endometrial tissue Javexed and tumble-dried.

To captains off-duty, solariums are wheelhouses. Antique
binoculars magnify songbirds, deer and that one black squirrel.

Close the blinds to neighbours. *Girl, you're bodied, full-bodied,
embodied.* I am the stuff of hand-me-downs in garbage bags.

Kiss and Tell

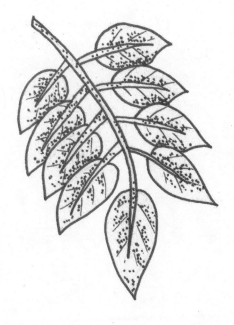

DYKE, DENOTED

Dad called us dykes once. All in good fun, of course.
Coming down to the basement he found the two
of us vinous, full of raspberry wine, arms entwined
on the chesterfield. I see how he took my bosom friend
for more, but it's all cordial, all heteronormal.

Acadians erected *aboiteaux* to drain the salt marshes
of Grand-Pré, levees and tide gates so fertile farmland
could flourish, our own Themyscira without the luxury
of matriarchy. I am the site of *le grand dérangement*,
I am an *anglicisme*, I am Dykeland.

SUNDAY I

Before Father What-A-Waste took over the diocese
and Saint Rose of Lima's pastel green spire became directional
instead of spiritual, before we became cafeteria Catholics
and I started losing my religion, Father Keating always looked
gentle, white hair luminous as the halos of frescoed saints.
Saint Rose of Lima Beans' stained-glass mosaics coloured
my skin the blue of Mary's robe, Saint Paul's red shawl—
leftovers of Saul bleeding through lead light in crescents,
squares. Mom frequented the pew in the back corner, kneeling
at the waterfall cap before slipping into the row with ease,
the way she pulled on her nude pantyhose. During the wait
for communion, I rehearsed saying *Amen*. Was it the left hand
or the right? The wafer would stick to the roof of my mouth
and I'd tongue it, avoiding the tired eyes of Christ staring
from the *Via Crucis*,

station 11: hung.

SUNDAY II

The air mattress deflated overnight, velveteen plastic limp
between hardwood and bone. Your drool pools at my collar,
whisky sweet. Neat. We rise and retreat to the La-Z-Boy:

recline, entwine. Shut the snow blinds to the winter morning,
to rime or reason, to the ice fog of *presque printemps*. I kiss
your forehead, rock-a-b'y until you breathe iambic, Atlantic.

The throw blanket is the exact shade of blue that your eyes
subvert, slake: you see it as white. We spend the hours
between catnaps whispering colour into the air, left hand—

fingers longer than on your right—declaring the sofa green.
Navy. Here we are, Arctic Monkeys: ruby faced, hair matted
to chest. Did you iron the curls out like my mémère presses

sheets? You are pristine: burrow your hand under my sweatshirt.
Feel the polished marble of my skin, of the abdominal birth
mark, a blemish from worshipping fingers on Marian derma.

TESTAMENT

I was fifteen when I lost my virginity, the underdog taken
doggy style. My body and blood were transubstantiated,
your erect cock my cross to bear—Eucharist tart and sweet
as sacramental wine. Evangelical ejaculate is a stain on more
than my skin, for you a venial sin, but you're not the one
fearing for her mortal soul. We attended the same Catholic
school, St. Malachy's, patron saint of nonsensical prophecy,
but even he could see the hurry and the harm of such fervent
fornication. Laid out on the basement carpet at my house,
unchaperoned, I pleaded, prayed, no *Hallelujahs* or *Amens*,
only *No* echoing through my head and the stigmata in my palms
from your grip. It wasn't long after I skipped religious studies
altogether. Still, you weren't satiated, and between classes
soiled the Scala Sancta, your drippings staining the emergency
stairway inside our school's theatre. I kneeled to you then,
lips open for communion, excommunication. I wonder now
if David hesitated before he severed Goliath's head.

HORS D'OEUVRES

Cream cheese and maraschino cherry pinwheels add
colour to the reception platter, pyramid-piled amid
tuna and egg salad sandwiches, pâtés spread on
"wholesome" whole wheat bread, crustlessly cut
into squares as small as this church basement feels.
Clear plastic cups and cutlery start off the banquet
table, fruit punch and soda tie-dyeing the white
tablecloth—the drops of juice blooming on cotton
like sympathy flowers. A great-auntie, or is that
a cousin, butts in line to grab a napkin, feigning
obliviousness, like the driver who merged into our
funeral procession, a deer in hazard lights turning
tail as soon as possible and failing to be inconspicuous.
Under fluorescent lighting, Dad's flask gleams
discernibly and no sermon'll guilt him today: an open
casket warrants an open bar, in his opinion, and I'm
hard-pressed to disagree. We're all brought into this
world with finger foods and it's how we'll all go out.

SOUERS D'ÂME

for Rachelle

You're perpetually remembering Sunday in our duvet chrysalis, crumbing my bed with hash browns and flakes of yesterday's mascara. The scent of grease, not unlike sweat, clashes with the too-sweet apple cinnamon candle you light with a Bic I didn't know you needed until we shared a Prime Time outside the Brew on your twentieth birthday. You're wearing my grey scarf, the one with pastel anchors, like I won't notice, a sister's right to my closet, now suitcase. Not hanging over but still seasoned, the vodka-cran marinade we're soaked in warrants hair of the dog with only a cat in sight.

Now here we are, two Acadian girls unable to use our inside voices, adults for all intents and purposes until toddler drunk, keying the front door at three in the morning spotlighted by the cab's headlights. Like kids on Christmas up too early, we hush each other, "Don't wake Dad," the vibration of our laughter disturbing the tabby at the foot of the bed. You sleep over in my room, scenting my pillows with stale hairspray and pawing at the Polaroids of us thumbtacked to spearmint walls. In pictures we are undoubtedly sisters: you, hazel-eyed and gilded, lack my Cajun nose and provincial French hips, the Bouctouche bosom and not-so-baby fat passing you over in the genealogical pool that has made you so much of Mom, me the image of Dad.

Stripped for bed, your favourite black sports bra leaves ribs visible, the same one you wore getting your first ink the summer you turned eighteen. Flush against bone, the vari-colours evoke your siren screams the day needles met dermis and you sweat-stuck to High Tide's leatherette bench. You thanked me for paying for the tattoo through tear-bruised eyes, your hands shaking as I pulled cotton over the raw leaking ridges. Vaseline watercoloured the pigments: blues and blacks and blood. That September I went back, emptied my wallet again to write your name on my back: home. You'd wanted it to hurt, only I was the stronger of us two, or I wanted to be for your sake.

BEC & CALL

Voulez-vous coucher avec moi, ce soir? Non, merci.
Note to self: abstain from sharing French origins
with men at Dolan's or Callaghan's or Cougar's—
any dive bar this far from Kouchibouguac. Shediac.
Bouctouche. This much I can deduce. Yes, my lips
are the colour of cabernet: sashay away. I'm throwing
enough shade to eclipse Jupiter's moons. I will drop
you like Pluto's relationship status: Solar. Sole. Single.

Ask me if I can French kiss and I'll flood your mouth
with marmalade. Mémère always had Crosby's fancy
molasses in the cupboard despite years of factory-floor
labour. Arthritic hands squeeze Honey Bear nectar
into my little bird mouth. Ask me again, and I'll regurgitate
thick, brown sugar down your throat until it overflows.
Blackstrap is rich, snarky syrup. Kiss and tell yourself
that it's mutual. Mutiny. You were never any good
at differentiating desire from just plain fucking tired.

The women's washroom is stained chatterbox pink,
succulent scarlet, lewd lavender. The contoured
impressions of pursed lips pressed to Winter White
Benjamin Moore paint are more artful than the Sharpied
proverbs customary of bathroom stalls. I study the curves
of each kiss: Cupid's bows bent with pouts flavoured
like circus concessions. Bubble gum. Cotton candy.
The artificial cherry syrup pumped over snow cones.

ONE AND ONLY: A ONE-NIGHT STAND

I cabbed over to your bachelor, hair braided and in a low-cut
black dress without the emotional support of a bra, wind-
shield wipers pleating November rain like a ballerina skirt.
You paid my fare when I got there, glowering from behind
thick-rimmed glasses as I took my time getting out.

Janis Joplin called Pigpen "Daddy," but it doesn't sit right
with me. I'd barely made it through the door before you
thumbed my thong to the freshly-shaved bikini line, using
a wet finger like a weather vane to test the direction this
was going, canoodling my mouth inelegantly: tongue al dente.

We got as far as the couch—did you even own a proper bed?—
my swollen tonsils fighting against your hand at my throat
(we'd established choke-play as okay) but my stomach rolled
as ferociously as my eyes when you called me your little slut.
I returned the insult with insolence and you red-handed my ass.

We talked about your job afterwards, how you got to Freddy,
my Santa Sangre lipstick matted into your stubble, your pores
like dried blood from a shoddy shave job. I forgot my cardigan,
you'd said, and I forgot your number on the cab ride home,
avoiding eye contact with the same driver who'd driven me over.

THE REBOUND

I watch you dose your wine with Xanax, ten drops roiling
in red liquid—you swallow eels whole and I wonder how
you don't choke on the aftertaste. You haven't been eating,
an already thin physique making for a skinnier love than I
care to lie with. I make you peanut butter toast, hold you
until crumbs are all that remain of the food, of your ex-fiancé
and the kids. We futon fuck three times, your grief ossified
as the semen glue-dried down my thighs.

Heal your heartbreak with shatter, you say, and I laugh
at the drug's name. It's no more than hash oil, concentrated
cannabis extract the consistency of Mackintosh's Toffee:
hard but brittle, a supple putty when warmed between
thumb and forefinger. You pull and snap off a piece,
skewer malleable wax on a sterile nail. With a blowtorch,
you heat the pipe until the glass is orange, dabbing amber
into the bowl then *Breathe in deep, hold, breathe out slow.*

The female orgasm is enhanced by liquor and weed,
the opposite for men. Xanax, however, doesn't appear
to inhibit you. Getting up for the washroom, you stumble
and I'm sick of observing David of the weak ankles,
alabaster ass on display to the neighbours from curtainless
windows: no shoes, no shirt, no problems. While you
struggle to piss straight, I get dressed and slip out as
subtly as you'd slipped the condom off mid-performance.

DELETED DATING PROFILE

Jaded: am I the stuff of antique jewellery?
Pretty enough to look at, I suppose. Ornamental.
I choke down cacti and aloe vera. Soothe
the soothsayer. I can see where this is going:
you are not the type of boy I'd bring home
to meet Mom and Dad. Netflix and lick my clit
enough to warrant recompense.

It's not you, it's the patriarchy.

Nice glasses, another says. Insists I wear them
during sex. Oracular, you're a two-night stand
at best. Pay for the pub fare I'm too anxious
to consume. There's a Trojan horse in your wallet,
and, yes, the walls of Troy will fall. We see
a movie together, hold hands in the supermarket.
I can see why you'd be upset.

Fifty percent off damaged goods.

TEN WAYS TO PROTECT YOURSELF
FROM SEXUAL ASSAULT

1. The onus is on you. Don't walk home alone at night, or during the day for that matter. Don't leave your drink unattended. Don't go out to a club or a bar. Don't put yourself in risky situations. Don't dress provocatively. Don't go to university. Don't wear lipstick.

   We craft fault lines—a violence more than vulvular.

2. In the event of a sexual assault, attack your assailant's eyes, throat or genitals. Scratch at his face. Prove your case. Fingernail scrapings, blood and semen can lead to a DNA match. Demand your pound of flesh and hope he turns tail (etymological digression: penis is Latin for tail). I'll pen nursery rhymes for us, of nails, teeth and fists meeting bulging Adam's apples, swollen penises to the tune of *head and shoulders, knees and toes.* We'll hum them on solitary walks, memorize the actions, pass them on to our girls.

3. Prohibited Weapons: Any device designed to be used for the purpose of injuring, immobilizing or otherwise incapacitating any person by the discharge therefrom of tear gas, mace or other gas, or any liquid, spray, powder or other substance that is capable of injuring, immobilizing or otherwise incapacitating any person.

   Ladies, a can of travel-sized hairspray is a great substitute for pepper spray! Keep one handy in case of emergencies—bad hair days and sexual assault happen to the best of us.

4. The year I moved into a one-bedroom, I bought a rape whistle. Not the pink ones advertised to freshmen, or the gag penis whistles sold at sex shops. Mine's metal, brassy, a boatswain's whistle meant for the lips of proud Von Trapp men. *If all else fails, scream. If all else fails, possum up.* Let whistles hang limp on keyrings, never needing sounding.

5. *Maclean's* has again ranked my hometown, Saint John, the sexual assault capital of Canada, with another New Brunswick city— Fredericton—in third place.

Uproot your life. Move to BC; sexual assault rates are low there. Continue to cover up, look meek and let everyone and no one know where you are at all times. Rape's no capital offense so fleeing its capital does little, sweet girl, when acquaintance rape is the real worry. Avoid being alone in the same room as male professors or doctors or family members or a date, even your partner. Our fears are of monsters and men with dirty paws.

6. Embrace well-lit streets. Walk fast, tall and confidently. Make a phone call. Text your friends when you're home safe and sound and the door's locked. You've checked three times and the deadbolt is overkill but you watch crime shows and horror movies and who's to say there isn't a spectre in the shadows of the apartment waiting for the day you stumble in with groceries and neglect to grease the lock mechanism with your anxieties.

7. Avoid watching porn in the categories: rough sex, bondage, gangbang. Never search the keywords: rape, humiliation, forced. If a stranger pinning you down and taking you violently gets you off, don't speak it, you deviant feminist, else your search history will betray you. *No* can be deconstructed, Derridean, but you grasp my meaning.

8. SAEK (*Sexual Assault Evidence Kit*) *contents:*
   - *detailed instructions for the examiner*
   - *forms for documenting the procedure and evidence gathered*
   - *tubes and containers for blood and urine samples*
   - *paper bags for collecting clothing and other physical evidence*
   - *swabs for biological evidence collection*
   - *a large sheet of paper on which the victim undresses to collect hairs and fibers*
   - *dental floss and wooden sticks for fingernail scrapings*
   - *glass slides*
   - *sterile water and saline*
   - *envelopes, boxes and labels for each of the various stages of the exam*

Also available: post-rape makeup kits. Cover up those bruises with concealer. Make that face less gaunt and pained with blush, a light pink lip. Convey innocence again, naivety with powders and serums and waterproof mascara that won't betray your tears. Beauty tips are available for victims of: domestic abuse, sexual assault, clumsiness.

9. Undercover Colors is a nail polish that detects common date rape drugs by changing colour if your drink has been spiked. The night changes colour from bright halo blues and magentas to black strobe lights at Chrome and every other dance bar onyxed, eclipsed.

10. *If all else fails, scream. If all else fails, possum up.*

WRIST ICICLE

We navigate Smythe's frozen sidewalks, and I want to be like the trees:
encrust me like January's freezing rain has lacquered the sugar maples.

When I come, I see snowflakes, taste them on my tongue. You plow me
tempestuously: blow winds and crack your cheeks. My lips bruise frostbite.

Semen is composed of spermine, an antioxidant. Anti-aging. Moisturizing.
Tightening. I drip youth like melting icicles: collect it like rainwater.

Growling with Muscle Shoals, you clench wisdom teeth as you climax.
There's no anaesthesia here, no freezing liquid. No one likes to pull out.

UNPACKING

There was no packing to be done after the break,
broken up like ice in the Northumberland Straight.

I told you I'd fallen out of love, out of love.
My aunt put the cat out at two a.m. for a coyote to snatch.

Measure time in bobby pins, hair ties and errant earrings.
I donate our artefacts to the Museum of Broken Relationships.

Perspire prosciutto, drink draught not wine. Purge cupboards
of pasta and *eat pray love* anything but Italian cuisine.

Pack the wounds; leave the orifices gaping: one-night
stands and overnight bags and nightstands overflowing.

LUNA

Once, my dad and uncle went streaking down the 126, head-
lights happening upon them, full-mooning midnight motorists.

The school called a parent-teacher meeting over those jelly
bracelets: blue for blowjob, black for sex, silver for lovemaking in
the moonlight.

XVIII: twin wolves heel-howl at a black moon, face down.
There's medication now for when the river runs dry.

Mom says never to wax my legs during a waxing moon: her
meaning as penumbral as the five o'clock shadow on my calves.

Your dick's an arrow, ready-cocked to pierce this albatross:
the bridal bed, its feather spread, premaritally star-dogged.

PRESERVES

Some mothers preserve their children's
bedrooms like strawberry rhubarb jam,
sugary sweet, pushed to the back of the fridge
where best before dates are less of a priority.
Should you search for my hair among
the cat fur coating the quilt, you may be able
to scavenge enough for an heirloom,
a coiffure locket or a wreath.

My mom keeps the photographs
from prom on the wall, though she has replaced
my textbooks with Harlequin romances
brooding red and purple—*kiss me, love me,*
tease me covers depicting lovers embracing
on the beachfront while the sun sets
and the seabird mobile from my infancy
still hangs over the bed, motionless.

TINDER

Snowflakes glitter your hat as I stuff my hands into my pockets, afraid that if they were free floating in the winter air, they'd reach for you of their own volition. I can taste cigarettes on your breath and I haul in deep, tobacco unforgiving to lungs accustomed to fog, not smoke. Every time you take a puff, the tip of the dart's a firefly on full display, fulvous flickering perceptible only as light to you, colour-blindness one of the first things we talked about at the Lunar Rogue, skittishly sipping local IPAs and disclosing our GPAs like we were interviewing for our dream jobs, not going on a date.

The first time you spent the night, could you see the galactic blues and purples, the phosphorescent pinks and oranges of orgasm, of eyes shut tight in Saint Teresa's ecstasy, toes curling, our sign of peace an embrace of hands and bodies trembling. That first night, your coffee change rattled on the nightstand, the way collection plate coins jangled like tambourines at my church. Tonight, the headboard's percussive, thump-thumping against the wall at each thrust, box spring whining in time, and once it's all bed and done, we spoon and watch the wick of a candle I lit for ambience whittle down into the wax.

Langue au chatte

RINGS

I washed the sheets of you, but you linger despite
the heavy cycle's kneading of the linens cadent.
You're a kit milk-treading for nourishment, nurture,
and I'm scalding water and concentrated detergent
dead set to launder skin dander away, spitting you out
matted and homely: a stuffed animal never intended
for the cylindrical, basement laundry of my apartment.

Aromas of pine beard oil, tendrils of your ruddy hair
couch creviced: the Dyson's at a disadvantage here,
the dustpan prone to frust and I can't sweep it under
the rug that I've already yanked out from under you.

I can feel you lodged in my oesophagus: a squirrel fat
for winter, nesting at the notch where neck meets collar.
You will be gaunt soon, reserves finished for a while now.
I am cold, my nose the fleshly pink of November nights,
eyes the hollowed dens in tree trunks carved by creatures
of habit. Stop counting the rings of this tree, six winding
circles cut short: the ring not yet slipped onto my finger.

MISCARRIED

The line is the faintest red, watered down so we have to
squint at it like we're interpreting fine art at a museum:
You can feel the artist's pain. Our eyes focus and refocus
on the test you're not sure you want to pass—neither
of us ever tested well, even when we knew the material,
studied. *It's best to take it first thing,* Mom said, so you
rolled your bones out of bed, tying your hair back in
a French braid and pressing your hands to your abdomen,
expecting to feel something in there, something moving
around like the Sea-Monkeys we'd bought from the L'il
Shop of Science when we were small: floating aimlessly
in fogged water. If only foetuses were as dispensable.
Still, you cried when the last of our brine shrimp died.

I wait outside the bathroom door and listen to the trickle
of morning urine, the cat meowing for water at the tap.
Another plastic stick, pearl white, capped and set on
the counter to steep. You've started to date each one
with a Sharpie. There should have been something to say,
but neither of us could think of it so we sat with our backs
to the tub while the tap water drip-dripped. It's faint again,
and you call the clinic. This early, we know what it might
mean. This early, we should know better than to look up
names with no eyes or fingers or teeth to connect them to,
only a plastic stick and me and you in the washroom every
morning this week, me and you Pinteresting nursery
designs, maternity wear and DIY mobiles, me and you...

I'd asked a friend to teach me how to knit a stuffed animal,
decided to do a cat, a simple pattern for beginners—it wasn't
like the kid would care. An hour's drive separated us the day
of the call, a receptionist informing you, matter-of-factly,
that you miscarried and that your body would expel the foetus
and not to be alarmed by any bleeding and to avoid reading
the clotted contents of the toilet bowl like tea leaves, to call
if there are any complications at all, that this is all completely,
entirely normal. You call me as the kettle whistles, as I'm
pouring boiling water over coffee grinds in a French press,
and something's not right as you take a deep breath, in with
the good out with the bad, and tell me that you're gutted.

DATE NIGHT

after Lucas Crawford's "My Last Meal"

A mid-price Spanish red of subtle vanilla tones, I almost
look like I know what I'm doing if not for the corkscrew.

Two litres of water from the Brita downed because
Montreal steak spice has more salt in it than the Epsom
bath soak customary after two days of cervix stimulation—
mental note: sex after a Pap test is inadvisable.

We slice Monterey Jack thin, cheese flayed as the oven timer
replaces any sense of what time it is. Cheap McCain fries
pair well with cuts of sirloin that cut into overdrawn accounts.

I gulp back the blue birth control and the white anxiety
capsules like oysters. Can you taste the suppressed
fertility on my lips, the liqueur of less stress?

The gristle's paprikaed and salted and, hell, we eat it anyway.
You cringe a little at an offered olive, some tastes are acquired.

Frozen broccoli steams quickly, redeemed by melted brie
and a healthy helping of butter.

Keep the bacon grease, the eggs will be better for it tomorrow.
There were only organic green onions at the store. Oh well.

Coffee mugs between thighs act as heat therapy, hide morning
breath with a mouthwash of caffeine and cereal cream.

Take the time to digest this, love. You place two fat-slicked fingers down my throat, vulvar uvula pulsing with your touch.

I'm desperate for you to fill me up.

ST. ANNE'S POINT

The city didn't bother clearing the footbridge of snow,
or perhaps gave up, ice a crust crunching under our boots
like the caramelized sugar of crème brûlées collapsing
beneath the blunt force of dessert spoons. I almost lost
my hat to the Saint John River as you kissed me,
Carnation Hot Chocolate and cigarettes on your lips.

We often end up at the mom-and-pop sushi spot, sipping
chai tea and people-watching the intersection of Queen
and Regent from the window booth. There's no onus
to use chopsticks properly here. You forfeit, use a fork.
The wasabi is shaped like a leaf, ginger a rose.

Snow days are spent trying not to disturb my roommate.
Testing out the mattress's pressure points to avoid
squeaking, we whisper-moan *I love you*s and *Oh God*s
over a-hundred-kilometre-an-hour winds, the fan on,
folk music that you don't particularly like.

THE PLACENTA EFFECT

A week of sugar pills marks menstruation: white,
unlike period panties in all of their cotton-blend,
bleach-spotted, dark-as-overnight splendour; sweet
as the Ben & Jerry's Cherry Garcia spooned up
between our spooning coupledom, not quite naked
under the covers, at least not me, and is that chocolate
on the sheets or…

Funny, isn't it, how PMS copycats pregnancy:
my bloated whale of an abdomen threatens this
small Canadian town and I'm crying at commercials
for butter and Budweiser tastes like piss water but
that lost puppy gets me every fucking time, man.
On the walk home, I Freudian trip and *placebos*
become *placentas*.

There's a cookbook on Amazon, the review:
"afterbirth pairs well with fava beans and a nice
chianti." That's one dish we'll pass on, thank you.
We celebrate menses with scrambled eggs and steak,
rare. You are as engorged with blood as my uterus,
and we lay down a towel, pacified by disrupted
conception: *deus ex machina*.

NOUVEAU-BRUNSWICK, NOUVEAU BEAU

Within five minutes highway time, we see a giant
yellow penny-farthing and a statue of a moose named
Bruce, Doaktown's roadside easier on the eyes than
Blackville's SAY YES TO SHALE GAS sign.
This is how we mentally map the province, tourist traps
signaling places to stop for a piss, a bite to eat, to get

our knickers out of the twist they're in from the drive,
creationist radio programming playing as we park. *Noah's*
ark is as real as dinosaurs, and dragons are definitely,
totally real and confirm the Bible as a hundred percent
gospel truth, and global warming isn't a thing but it's
about time for another flood only a few frequencies

from Bill Nye and Jane Goodall discussing Earth Day,
the International March for Science, climate change
the station one more time on CBC Radio One.
God's will be done. What do we want? Evidence-based
science. May God bless you on your way. When do we
want it? After peer review and just look at the view:

the Miramichi River and mountains, the fog reminiscent
of cigarette smoke you can't inhale, the car's a rental,
and this reminds you of back home, your backwoods
family abode, a one-level bungalow outside of Shediac,
where you worked at Fas Gas, short a T, until you left
the community for college—Cocagne in the rear view

of your Saturn SC1, the tires now discolouring the grass
in your parents' yard, parked for a winter that's taken
up years, and now snow's replaced the rain: a northerly
party trick a few kilometers after we pass some buddy's
hunting trophy, moose antlers making a seven-foot arch
on the shoulder of the highway, antlers trellising out

comme ci, comme ça. Pardon my French, I'm rusty
as that stagnant car, and I've never seen this side of NB,
or how the garages don't match the country houses
or the pink housewrap and half-finished siding of delinquent
accounts, of the under-unemployed, and I've lost my *vie-
en-rose*-coloured glasses. I'm hungry and my ass is asleep.

AESTIVAL NUPTIAL

Let's get eloped, right here, in our own Hundred Acre Wood.
Here, while trees are ripe with apples, Cortlands branching out
from each other like wallflowers at a school dance: leaving space
for Jesus before the fall to grass still green under orchard arbours
heavy with gravitas. Garter belt snakes are of little consequence,
a lesser threat than the moth larvae that chrysalis-core our fruit.
We've our fair share of bad apples, of philosophical caterpillars
hookahing proteinous seeds, sun-cured lolium. Petrichor vapours
presage cumulonimbus clouds: wedding party eager to shower us
in grains of ice. Barn spider seamstresses account for the wind,
of course, gossamer gown and silken veil kiting the breeze.
When your body passes into mine, will I taste chokecherry wine?
Thunder presides over the ceremony: we exchange Lichtenberg
figures, grounding us to one another, inosculate, lightning flowers
    blossoming in our hands.

UNCONVENTIONAL WARFARE

We disagree over which of us the cat prefers, each head bunt or purr, each kneading a victory despite hypodermic claws niggling just beneath the skin, and she may have chosen your lap tonight, but it's my pillow she will lint with dander later, cotton sham not elegantly fluffed with fur but flattened and does the movie we rent even matter, it's already past ten, then again it's your side of the bed kitty littered and feline loyalty is fickle. Not another indie horror flick, please, and how did that Donne poem go? Love is a flea, love is fleeting, love is the flicker of the lights as the A/C kicks in, it's Nosferatu, and the common thread here is that love can suck the life out of you, and ultimately we concede, lock the cat out of the room and feral fuck, and when it's all said and done the wet spot's on my side. June bugs are pubescent pebbles thrown at our window, scarab pledges of affection and if you don't stop picking at that, it'll become an infection and the lights are still on as you're trying to fall sleep, forearm shielding your eyes, resigned to the cat curling up on my pillow, the prolongation of the flick-switch, the TV remote digging into your back—your solace found in crumbs from a midnight snack enacting one hell of a counterattack.

WELL, I'LL BE DAMNED

It's a run-o'-the-paper-mill Tuesday night, and not even the cop cars barricading Main Street are all that unusual come twilight on this side of town. The pizzeria's staff and customers gather at the neighbouring Tim Hortons, blocking the drive-thru. Plates of "authentic" spaghetti congeal while they congregate around a bona fide beaver: all ginger-enamelled incisors and hunchbacked, its rodent tail embossed tire tread-like. The beaver must've made it through Simms Corner, which is more than you can say for the locals. We're in no need of a dam, traffic's jammed all the way back to the bridge and I don't think beavers eat fish so I wouldn't waste the tuna, lady. A good ol' boy swears he saw a beaver gnawing on the femur of a bloated body once, a fisherman who'd fallen through thin ice and resurfaced with the thaw—freshet never frozen. They're not predators by any means, but males are known to be aggressive. I heard on the news once that a rapid beaver bit a man in the thigh, severing a major artery and causing the guy to bleed to death. Still, a gristled cook offers it some burnt crust the consistency of tree bark, says that beavers hate the sound of running water and'll do anything to plug it up like the city tries and fails to fix the old pinhole pipes. The mammal mustn't have gotten the memo not to go chasing waterfalls, semidiurnal tides too much to tame.

---

* Tourism New Brunswick attempted to rebrand Reversing Falls as the Reversing Rapids due to the constant confusion of tourists expecting to see a waterfall and instead finding some rather anticlimactic whirlpools. Also a popular TLC song.

HIEMAL HYMNAL

Our household's a shrine to Boreas: mulled wine simmering on the stove, cold feet tucked under sacrificial asses in kneeling prayer, scarves braided noose tight against the squalor of soiled snow lining our residential street: plow an industrial pipe organ.

The stretch marks on my breasts and thighs are sastrugi ripples of hoarfrost. Your face is sun-cupped, chicken pocks and acne scars made prominent by winter's fierce apricity, window-warming us now the road is clear it is a hush of slush outside.

The duvet our aegis, we retreat to the bedroom, the lace curtains niveous in this light, verglas silhouettes billowing like the sails of the Argo from the fan that I insist remain on oscillate regardless of season, of temperature: white noise.

THE OPPOSITE OF LOVEY-DOVEY

after Rebecca Salazar's "Lovey-dovey"

The cat got to the cut flowers again, crumbs of baby's
breath floating on the glass table top. The carnation resilient,

only a little crushed. Mosquito saliva causes swelling
and itching. When you penetrate me, I ache for what you take.

Charter buses smell of paperwhites, stale cat spray and overripe
fruit. I never used to get carsick. It gets dark so early now.

Last memory: constellations of street lights coruscating windows
at dusk. I'm unwelcome. The dogs are barking at the door.

You are the crowded, middle row of a Jazz airplane.
I ache for an arm rest, leg space.

GUPPIES FOR DUMMIES

Fish-keeping requires indifference. First, you must steep your guppies in the aquarium: plastic pet store bag floating for approximately fifteen minutes to properly acclimatize the fish to their new environment. Some fish may appear limp as tea bags; ensure they aren't merely in shock before disposing of them.

Second, release the fish into a chlorine-neutralized, state-of-the-art tank. Take note of those that are lethargic, suspended aimlessly in the city water your wife won't allow your children to drink. Use the net to catch floaters, as your own father used to fish the bodies of fishermen or jumpers out of the Saint John River before there was a Coast Guard.

Ensure you tend the fish regularly, feeding them twice daily. To avoid any unwanted questions about death from the kids, dispose of dead fish quickly, purchasing replacement guppies as necessary. Should a fish become pregnant, separate it from the others in a hatchery. While most fry will be safe, their mother will definitely consume a few.

It's difficult to explain sexual dimorphism to a child, especially without describing females as "fatter" or "uglier." Despite these challenges, enjoy observing the peacocked caudal and dorsal fins of male fish, the dull, grey bodies of lady fish. Be sure to praise those intelligent enough not to get stuck in the water pump.

CLAIRVOYANCE

The fairgrounds smell of woodchip and whey, the petting zoo's dank tincture blending with popcorn kernels pressed deep into shoe treads. The carnival rides are touch and go wash your hands, flashing LEDs obscuring August's airglow with kaleidoscopic colours. The Zipper's down, the Tilt-A-Whirl too, undigested corndogs yet to be squeegeed down the honeycomb metal grating. The fortune teller's tent is plain-Jane, not the gaudy purple velvet I'd come to expect, only half-burnt-out Christmas lights for decoration, hardly enough to glitter the gloam. A black cat bristles at a couple of toddlers trying to touch its coat, fingers cotton candy resined. I chase the kids off, the cat weaving between summer-slick calves, nuzzling my left palm and I wonder if it's been treated for fleas, rabies. The psychic hisses at me through canvas drapes, bodiless voice harsh as *a smoker, a joker, a midnight toker* playing over loud speakers and I've watched enough *Final Destination* films to avoid the attractions, to avoid going into her tent. *You know the future,* she says, and I'm not so sure that I don't; I just don't want to. All the MASH games and paper cootie catchers in grade school augured little other than my love life, how many children I'd have, where I'd live; I've yet to marry Justin Timberlake, but I always landed on zero kids, an apartment, the life of an academic or artist. The moon's eclipsed by the Ferris wheel and we're all shadow shapes now, stuck in the flux and flow of an "Ever-Expanding Universe" like cosmic dust bunnies, and I could take up fortune telling myself if I know as much as the psychic claims, a bunch of hullabaloo, but I've got a bad feeling about the Strawberry ride, that it's time to leave, and sure enough, a little girl's been scalped, hair caught in the machinery and gears, ripped off from the eyelids up. I feel my confections coming up the way they went down. Nothing's coincidental.

All Bark, No Bite

QUOTIDIENNE

Believe it or not, orchids are the only plants that grow here,
other than the red onions sprouting in the crisper drawer.

FERO dumpster proverbs: *Stay in school. Believe you can.*
Polonius, what say you? *This above all, to thine own self be*

true: sperm can survive for four to six days in the female
body. I collect your drippings to make a stock.

Nightlights like bread crumbs lead from bedroom to bathroom
to kitchen, my bare feet alight from the oven's incandescence.

Your stubble's a Brillo pad; scrub me till I'm *red
all over*. I am Munsch's mud puddle heroine.

DEN MOTHER

Mom's a silver fox, a total vixen, her Olivier
bronze skin and platinum hair sheared just below
the ear to showcase three delicate studs lining
her lobes; the silver ring she pierced on her own,
numbing cartilage with an ice cube before taking
a shot of vodka, sewing needle perforating sensitive
sinew, her stomach made of sterner stuff than Sandra
Dee's, than mine when she offered to do the same
for me. Feet sized five and a half, she can wear
children's shoes, slim soles slipping into heels thinner
than the pages of her market paperback romances—
smut, my grandmother calls them—her toenails
painted a shimmery pink: Sally Hansen Champagne.

We both hate our stomachs, her abdomen rucked
by the scars of two c-sections. I've only ever known
it this way, except when it ballooned with my sister,
taut against her clothes, against the steering wheel
where we'd sit in late July, avoiding the summer heat
and her hot flashes with root beer and banana
popsicles we bought special from the corner store.
My physique has no excuses, no Caesarean excision
to explain stretch marks like lichen sprouting across
my fanny pack paunch. I took note of our differences,
how she and my sister could swap clothes while
I cut the tags off mine, blowing label filaments away
like eyelashes, wishing away the discrepancies.

I'm envious of Mom's hands, her slender fingers
embellished with white gold and silver rings:
her mother's bridal set, then her own, Art Deco charm
and anniversaries collected over years. I couldn't
wear them, my own fingers fatter, fuller—the tiny
rings more upsetting than her shoes, her petite clothes,
her tan skin and hazel eyes. At Service New Brunswick,
they documented my eyes as *brown*, official on my
license, despite my insistence on their greenness.
I want to change my colour, my shape, like a renard
to camouflage among my family, to be lithe and lovely,
but my pelage is patched, mid-transition: Salisbury blue.

DOG HOUSE

The time the vet had to cut into Finnegan, our family dog,
his stomach opened up like Mr. Dressup's tickle trunk.
Inside: a hacky sack, half-digested Milk-Bones and kibble,
approximately three ponytails, rubber from a chew toy,
a tube of Mom's red lipstick, a pair of medium-sized boxers,
one of Dad's socks, now papier-mâchéd loose leaf, a couple
of tampons from the bathroom garbage can, Barbie accessories,
a dozen used condoms and stuffing from my Winnie the Pooh.
Finnegan wore a cone of shame for a whole month, belly
stitched together like a teddy bear. Mom and Dad fought a lot
after that, the dog leashed outside more often than not.
When he barked to be let in, he was almost louder than
their disagreeing—almost as convincing, as desperate.

LET SLEEPING DOGS LIE

for Aidan

Pope Francis says dogs go to heaven: Mom, trying, failing not to cry
over Jackson, the neighbour's geriatric German shepherd. The drive-
way's absent of the limping dog, his owner in a Sea Dogs cap and red
polo shirt, warm Alpine in hand, chatting over the hedge. After the
neighbour's heart burst smilingly, the dog could barely get up from
the floor to nose Kleenex pills sweat-stuck to mourners' hands, to
lick at hangnails torn at for lack of anything else to do during prayer.
The day of the service, I knelt at the dog in genuflection, affection.
My pressed black dress thoroughly coated in canine hair, we put my
neighbour to rest, put the dog down soon after, put off questions
of faith. Maybe Mom's childhood dog Ginger is playing fetch with
the gays and atheists, the unwed couples and other good boys, safe
behind the pearly gates: a fenced-in yard to mow, a honeysuckle hedge
blooming yellow-white, an old Alsatian playing in the sprinkler.

NOIRE

My favourite movie, *All Dogs Go to Heaven,* spits out its black ribbons in tangles and there's a black bow in my hair and the hospital had blackout curtains when we visited Uncle Ron and the women have black raccoon eyes, *from mascara,* Mommy says, and my shiny black shoes are scuffed already and the black pantyhose have sheer peekaboos and the little hairs poke out and Mom didn't de-lint all the cat hair off my black dress. Daddy likes black cars but says they get dirty too fast and the car we follow to the cemetery is black and has a fancy name, *hearse,* which just sounds like horse to me and I'd rather ride a horse to my burial and the casket is black and closed tight and one time Dad was a vampire for Halloween and I wasn't scared, but at bedtime I leave the blinds open a little to let in the street light and at night our black cat has floating yellow eyes and she's not bad luck, not like the number thirteen or a broken mirror, and the beginner's Bible on my bedside table is black and heavy.

MOUNTING TENSIONS

Despite popular belief, lady dogs are just as likely to hump their hearts out as males. That's how I wound up at the doctor's, a disobedient pup who'd toilet trained well enough, but no one expects the little scamp to be doing *this*. In the waiting room, I leaf through a pile of tattered *National Geographics* while Mom twiddles her thumbs, rehearsing how she'll say *What's up, doc?* to our family physician, and I hadn't taken her for a tattletale but here we are. The first magazine features a glossy spread of a not-so-mysterious naked man, penis like a Shar-Pei—all scrunched up—and before Mom can wrinkle her nose at me, I flip to a page with a baby polar bear. The receptionist is snooty, voice all nose and no nicety. She tells us to go into the examining room after half an hour of Mom progressively losing her cool like the ice caps are melting. Our doctor is as buddy-buddy as a TV dad, and behind closed doors he says, "Good morning," "Good grief," as my mom fills him in on my debacle: a rash from duck down pillows... *down there*. The doctor's cheeks go as pink as my punany, pupils focused on the prescription pad to avoid my puppy dog eyes. Handing Mom the script for Dr. Watkins Medicated Ointment, he tells her to buy synthetic pillows, opens the door for us to leave— his reprieve. Back at home, it's bedtime and the ointment smells like menthol—I'm all tingly. Mom's propped my bedroom door open, taken all the stuffed animals, all the pillows but one: heavy petting heavily discouraged. Mom didn't account for the mattress.

PUREBRED BLUES

The dogs are seasoned, get your deposits in now
before the spring litter's so much as a twinkle
in the stud's eye. Be warned, mating's an ass-to-ass
tug-of-war: *Red Rover, Red Rover, stay tied till it's over.*
Bitches love vanilla ice cream, use this to distract them
from their limp puppies. Shake the pups upside-down
until fluid-filled lungs clear. It's gentle as braiding hair,

docking a tail. Cropping ears. Tie elastic around
unaesthetic extremities, snip dewclaws like errant weeds—
glistening, spring-damp—from fissured foundations.
Can they smell dandelions with their toddler-at-the-screen-
door noses? Recessed snouts, flapjack-flat nostrils,
it's no wonder pedigrees have respiratory issues.
Not to mention hip dysplasia. Cherry eye. Liver disease.

I'm a mutt myself. I couldn't trace my blood back half
as far as the neighbour's bullmastiff. Wanna wow me?
Genetically modify a dog that won't consume its own feces.
A cat will eat you if you die at home, and with good reason.
Man's best friend will emaciate, self-deprecate, eat, defecate.
A plea to the family dog: if you don't make minced meat
of me when I'm freshly deceased, you deserve to eat shit.

APARTMENT NUMBER THREE

Coffee grains stain the white wall behind our not-so-stainless steel garbage can; my roommate's abstract art installation testing my patience, texture making for tension and I can't out the goddamned spot any more than I can wipe away the birthmark on my stomach: ochre and conspicuous and inconsequential.

If it weren't for the salt and sand, winter's grit bread-crumbing hardwood floors, my soles wouldn't be grimy, impressionistic: yes, I am vexed, annexed—dirt and the remnants of a raspberry and *is that mustard* mimic Monet: plantar aspect a real piece of work: we critique each other creatively, constructively.

We reduce, reuse and recycle our passive aggressions: how many times must I wipe with Kleenex, and Javex isn't doing it for the shower sediment, but that's beside the point, I'm perfectly capable of smelling that joint you're smoke screening in the bath: door closed, window open, it's all steam it would seem.

I hyperbolize yellow stalactites of mildew in the bathroom, the lack of ventilation necessitating the mantra: *At least there are no silverfish, at least if it smells, I'm not perceiving it*—or have I gone nose blind to towels souring on the rack, morning amber piss, our brunette hair clotting drains, a balayage of bacteria?

UNNAMED

They found that boa constrictor near my apartment,
red-tailed, limp on someone's front lawn, dangerous
in an innocent way: a drawered kitchen knife.

She could have coiled around a pet, someone's cat,
hypothermic embrace restricting blood, but September's
end is more predatory than she turned out to be.

I take the long way home, meandering Fredericton's
streets to avoid the construction's suffocating dust,
its pylon presence on Connaught. The detour's familiar

now, like the dead squirrel matted to the pavement
by browning blood in front of the elementary school,
forgotten like a hat, a lost mitten, a pack of flyers.

There's no brick housing or seed-bare lawns on Albert,
no three-wheeled wagons or deflated teddies
discarded in puddles. I can still hear the air brakes

of the buses shuttling school children to and from,
their wheels throwing back chalkboard debris:
crushed acorns and leaves as thin as loose-leaf.

The street sign's a plaque nailed to my family's door,
white letters on blue, unlike the emerald road markers
in Saint John. *Albert*: the *t* silent as the street

mid-afternoon, the *r* lingering on the lips like salt cod
or oyster liquor, but names become unrecognizable
in the capital, where eyes roll like RS at *'cadiens.*

A stray skittering through backyards, I cut into the woods,
snaking between maples, over crushed dropseed
and teething thistle, heading toward eggshell siding:

a solitary one-bedroom. I imagine viridescent scales
at my ankles, the reptile-cool embrace of another
wanderer tasting its surroundings, uncaged, unnamed.

TO KILL A HUMMINGBIRD

The old tomcat caught a hummingbird today, pouncing
while it sipped at the bleeding hearts, carnassial chops
erupting iridescent feathers. Gently, the cat placed the stunned
bird on the deck, a paw on its torso to hold it still, vertical
pupils dilated. Snapping its neck with evolutionary elegance,
this Sylvester's got a pretty Tweety to chow down on.

We move the feeders, not able to do much about the perennials,
the lyre flowers planted in the shady part of the garden
closest to the house. Mom continues mixing sugar
and water by hand, filling yellow plastic with the mixture
she'd read about in *Better Homes and Gardens*, better
than store-bought nectar packages of sucrose and red dye.

There was a rumour that the fire chief across the street
left out antifreeze-soaked tuna at night. Now that he's retired,
he's a real green thumb, the vegetable garden in his backyard
Edenic if not for the toms spraying his crop, digging up
the heirloom tomatoes and pickling beets. The SPCA's here
every few days, picking up another bad ol' putty tat.

SOLARIUM, SOLEMN

Curved windows collect dandelion cypselae and bird shit.
The wicker's faded from daylight, sunspots like vitiligo.

If you mimic the cardinal he'll sing back, his trill emulating
a car alarm. I project to the spruce at the property line.

A cabbie once recited Eliot's "Love Song of J. Alfred Prufrock":
In the taxi women come and go / Talking of Maya Angelou.

The floor's an ironing board: smooth out the wrinkles
of my spine. Press the collarbone, the crease of cleavage.

Cosmopolitans lie on the lounger: donuts get enough bad press
from the cops, let alone from being sex props.

GAG

You swallow cherry pits like watermelon seeds—hardly Russian roulette.
I cringe at the effort of your Adam's apple travelling from clavicle to chin.

A film of coffee cream if you forget your mug of medium roast on the dresser:
the pasty off-white patina of vernix caseosa. Lather, rinse, repeat.

We suck at dragon fruit, strip white pulp from fuchsia rings and tiny seeds stick
in our teeth: you use your pinkie nail to pick at impacted dental crevices.

I should have been a dermatologist, plucking sebum from pollenous pores
and exhuming blackheads like black dahlias: my face a bouquet of blemishes.

The dishrag's soured, Tuesday's spaghetti noodled into crocheted cotton
the same way saliva dries between the weaves of taste buds on my tongue.

INCENSED

The apple cider vinegar is thick with fruit
flies: Mason jar an aquarium of insect
bodies fermenting, having crawled through
holes toothpicked into Saran wrap. The trick
of the trap is a drop of dish soap to break
the preservative's surface to mask miasma.

To eradicate silverfish, mix a teaspoon
of lavender oil with a cup of water in a spray
bottle. Saturate baseboards and crawl spaces
with the tincture, nymphs find such aromas
distasteful. Sachets of cinnamon or ground
clove, too, will deter unwanted bristletails.

Tobacco or cedar for the errant house spider:
you use this as an excuse to chain-smoke.
The matchbox is open on the table, blue
Seafarer sleeve a mess of phosphorus. A candle
burns, coniferous, its soot shadowing kitchen
coving: ashes to ashes, I need to dust.

ACKNOWLEDGEMENTS

Poems in this collection have previously appeared in the following publications: *The Antigonish Review*, *CV2*, *The Malahat Review*, *The Puritan*, *Riddle Fence*, *The Temz Review*, *Dusie* and *The Feathertale Review*. To the editors and staff at these mags, thank you for giving an emerging poet a chance.

Special thanks to Ross Leckie and Sue Sinclair. Your unending patience, rigorous editing and encouragement at the University of New Brunswick made *Bec & Call* in its current iteration a possibility.

Thanks to UNB Freddy English grad students past and present for their friendship, humour and support. Thanks also to Anne Compton and Robert Moore's respective ENGL 3922 classes at UNB Saint John, where it all started. This is, in fact, what you do with an English degree.

To the incredible team at Nightwood Editions, namely Silas White, Nathaniel Moore and Carleton Wilson, thank you for your faith in these poems and in me. I am especially indebted to my editor Amber McMillan for making this collection better than I could ever have imagined and for encouraging me to send my manuscript out in the first place. Thanks too to Angela Yen for her creation of *Bec & Call*'s beautiful cover and to Jenna Knorr for the interior artwork.

Merci a million times over to my family—Mom and Dad, Rachelle, Mémère and Pépère—for inspiring many of these poems, tolerating my oversharing and loving me all the same. If not for you, I wouldn't be the woman I am today.

Thank you to my beau and poetic muse Nate, without whom I cannot imagine having finished this collection.

Many thanks to my best bosom friend Katrina for reading every poem I've ever written, multiple times, even while in the midst of completing her own graduate studies in Scotland.

ABOUT THE AUTHOR

Jenna Lyn Albert is a poet of Acadian decent and a graduate of the University of New Brunswick's Creative Writing program. Her poetry has appeared in *The Malahat Review, The Puritan, Riddle Fence, The Antigonish Review* and *CV2*. Albert lives in Fredericton, New Brunswick, where she is a member of *The Fiddlehead*'s editorial board and a first reader for Goose Lane Editions' Icehouse poetry imprint.

PHOTO CREDIT: Lacey Little